Dear Judy,
Enjoy your ride with
Max!   Your friend,
                    Ed

FARES TO FRIENDS

FARES TO
FRIENDS

How to Develop
Outstanding Business Relationships

BY ED WALLACE

Ed Wallace, President
The Relational Capital Group
484-684-6270
edwallace@relcapgroup.com

Printed in the United States of America
First Edition

ISBN 978-1-4243-3102-4

Book Design by Kimberly Wallmeier
Illustrations by Jason Coleman

The caricatures throughout this book are not intended as actual depictions of the
persons represented.

For Laurie, Brett, and Grant,

My Best Friends

TABLE OF CONTENTS

PREFACE

The anonymous, popular nugget of business wisdom — "It's not what you know, it's *who* you know" — formed the basis for decades of books and workshops focused on networking as the key to successful sales and career management. Experience has taught me, however, that this adage is incomplete on two counts: 1) it undervalues the importance of knowledge and skills (a great list of contacts in your network will not help you much in the long run if you don't bring something of value to the table); and 2) it ignores a third, even more critical element in the equation — the *quality of your relationships* with people — in other words, the value of *How they know and regard you.*

My twenty-five years in the business world have led me to conclude that "who you know" may certainly be important but, by itself, is not enough of a strategy. It's based on a simplistic, dated, even quaint view of "getting ahead" in business — one that implies that patronage and opportunities for advancement are granted rather than earned, that an individual's own merit, character or attitude are less important than who they met at a cocktail party, their family connection to an executive or their acquaintance with celebrities. True, introductions and networks are vital, but decisions made based primarily on such factors don't necessarily result in sustainable value in the business relationship. In reflecting on my own experience, I am hard pressed to identify a single strong, sustainable and profitable business relationship that emerged only from "who I knew." Instead, outstanding business relationships have come from the manifestation of essential qualities like credibility, integrity and authenticity *experienced* in a business relationship — How each person knows and regards the other.

My passionate belief that this element is the most important piece of the puzzle is a conviction based on what I have found to be true for me. In the end, I find this a concept that is most compelling when shared on a personal, experiential basis. What I have to offer are the events of my own career and the lessons I learned riding in a British-style taxi driven by my mentor, my business guru, my good friend, Max.

What I hope you take away from Max and me is a sense of how important developing outstanding business relationships can be, in a way that has a clear, positive effect on your business performance, your career and your life.

PART I

My Friend Max

CHAPTER ONE

Fares to Friends

A number of years ago, my work required a significant amount of travel. I didn't like being away from my family any more than necessary, so I became king of the day-trippers. It got so that I could actually visit Minneapolis or Iowa for a meeting and still make it home to the east coast for a late dinner the same day. I would leave the house around 5 a.m. to drive to the airport and would return home in time to see Brett, our first child, for a few precious minutes before tucking him safely into bed.

The night before one of these trips, our car developed an engine problem. I asked my wife Laurie to reserve a taxi to the airport and as usually the case when she got involved, interesting events began to unfold.

The next morning at dawn I waited anxiously for the taxi to arrive, and the second the doorbell rang I ran to the door so the driver wouldn't ring a second time and wake our baby. When I opened the door, standing in front of me was a tall, lanky fellow with glasses and the sort of calm, kind face you might see in a classic Norman Rockwell painting. I was about to learn that this was not your average taxi driver. And by this, I don't mean to imply he was anything like the character "Jim" from the popular *Taxi* sitcom.

He greeted me courteously. I grabbed my briefcase, locked the door and began walking with him in the dark toward his parked taxi. I soon realized this was no ordinary taxi either. It was an old-style British taxi — 30 or 40 years old — with stately, rounded exterior lines, running boards, and a large rear passenger compartment. Even at 5:00 a.m., I could tell it was spotless. Climbing into the back, I settled into a luxurious leather seat, stretched out my legs, and felt a deep sense of comfort and relief. We began to drive and I noticed there was no noise — no scratchy dispatcher's voice barking instructions, no jangling music on the radio. A cooler within reach provided a supply of fresh drinking water. It was amazing!

As we pulled away, the driver turned around to introduce himself.

"My name is Max," he said with a smile.

"Glad to meet you Max," I said, and meant it. "My name is Ed."

"Nice meeting you, Ed."

As we drove, he asked me a couple of questions about myself. Since, like some people, I'm pretty much my own favorite topic, I was happy to oblige. He was a terrific listener and I found myself sharing a good deal about my life. He showed no trace of ego; he was completely focused on me. It was just him, me and the car, with no distractions. He took special note when I told him about our new young son.

For the next couple of weeks, when I needed a ride to the airport, we requested Max as my driver but found he was booked solid. After three or four tries, we finally got on his calendar with a good week's advance notice. Once again, I waited at dawn for the doorbell to ring. But this time, to my surprise, he merely tapped quietly on the screen door. He said he remembered we had an infant and knew that mom and baby needed all the sleep they could get.

During the next several rides to the airport in Max's marvelous taxi, we talked almost entirely about me and my life. (By now, you may have noticed that I was no longer driving myself to the airport). He asked about my work, where I was traveling to, my ambitions, my family. I could hardly believe how at ease I felt opening up to him.

Finally, I decided to ask him some questions for a change. So, he told me a few things about himself and his business, his day-to-day schedule as a taxi driver. He explained how busy he was and how he wished there was more time in the day so he could accommodate everyone who needed his services. He felt genuinely sorry he was unable to take care of them all.

His clients could not be easily categorized; they were all kinds of people. Businessmen like me going to the airport and elderly people going shopping. Groups of ladies going to the city for a day at the art museum, lunch, and a nice tour of the historic district, which Max was only too happy to provide. He didn't care who he was serving. Social status did not matter to him at all. To him, everyone was the same; he made no judgments. He had an interesting sense of peace about him.

Finally, I had to ask, "So, Max, how did you develop such a long list of loyal customers?"

"Simple, Ed," he said holding his thumb and index finger about an inch apart, "It's the little extras that turn fares to friends."

Customers as friends! What a concept.

I was sure I had heard something like this before, and quickly recalled an old commercial in which a company president hands out airline tickets to his employees in an effort to get them to reconnect with their customers face to face. He yearned for the time when business was built more on real relationships — even friendships — than on impersonal communication via phone, answering machines and faxes (and this was before cell phones, pagers and the Internet). Then, as the president himself begins to leave, an employee asks, "Ben, where are you going?" to which he responds, "Out to visit that old friend who just fired us!"

Over the past twenty years or so, it seems as though the art of developing business relationships has gotten lost in the barrage of sophisticated graduate school theories and the resulting management fads that have grown out of these theories. As much as cell phones and BlackBerry® devices can help keep us connected, they often serve as an additional barrier to real, in-person communication. Individuals we used to think of as business partners we now refer to coldly as "accounts" or, worse yet, "revenue streams."

If we lose sight of the fact that a *real person* is on the other end of that call or e-mail, then we miss the opportunity to enrich our business endeavors and our life with the growth and learning that comes from true interaction with others. Many people have taken the notion of work-life balance to mean that you only need to focus on the relationships in the "life" or personal part of that equation — when, in fact, there is tremendous gain to be had from treating your business relationships with as much care.

Just think about the possible benefits at work if you considered your business associates as friends just like you do in your personal life, just like Max did by offering the little extras that turned 'fares to friends'?

And what exactly were the 'little extras' that Max was talking about? Sure, it was great fun riding around in his taxi; it was the only one of its kind in the area and attracted a lot of attention. Still, this was only a small part of what made Max a success — and he *was* a success. If you paid close attention to this bespectacled sage behind the wheel, you could see that his entire business philosophy was based on friendship, and the 'little extras' that friends would do for each other.

Arriving on time. Courtesy and warmth. Impeccable upkeep of the vehicle. Providing a quiet atmosphere during the ride. The drinking water. The thoughtful interest in his customers' lives. The listening and the remembering. The gentle tap on the screen door at 5 in the morning.

I believe that Max woke up every morning, not thinking he was going to work, but rather that he was going to spend time with his close friends all day long — very different from the idea of business as a series of transactions in which both parties want something from each other. If we define friends as parties who *help* one another, and if you consider everyone you interact with as your friend, then you find it as easy to do the little extras in business as you do in your personal life.

On the simplest level, Max's job was to provide a ride from one place to another. Any driver could do that, and do it on time, safely and courteously. But, when you rode with Max, the quality of the relationship, the conversation — the whole experience — was so enjoyable, supportive, enlightening and pleasant that you just didn't want the trip to be over. By the time we arrived at the airport, I would have far preferred to stay in the taxi talking to Max and let the plane fly to Cleveland without me. He had mastered the art of taking his so-called simple business from a merely transactional level to the level of high-value personal relationships — creating a memorable experience between human beings.

Riding with Max off and on during those years opened my eyes to how poorly I was managing my own business relationships. With all due respect to the Rock Stars of Leadership (listed in the Appendix), Max was the greatest developer of business relationships and friendships that I have ever known. I learned more about developing and benefiting from these relationships by taking Max's taxi to the airport than I have ever learned from a course, a book or any other individual.

The rest of this book is devoted to exploring what it means to have real quality in your business relationships. In many ways, of course, doing this is its own reward, because quality relationships are satisfying, enriching, and they allow you to sleep well at night. Still, it's also undeniable that such relationships — such friendships — almost inevitably lead to rewards of the more ordinary sort - the kind that help to pay the mortgage and send the kids to college.

"It's the little extras that turn fares into friends!"

CHAPTER TWO

Mr. DeMarcantonio's Tomatoes and Dr. Fred

Laurie and I at one time had a neighbor named Mr. DeMarcantonio, who was not very friendly. He kept pretty much to himself, tending his vegetable garden, which came up to the edge of our driveway. He was outside in that garden every day from spring through summer, wearing a red baseball cap, digging, watering and generally occupying all of his time until fall. I had attempted, though somewhat half-heartedly, to hold conversations with him on several occasions, but I never got anything more than a strictly cordial "hello."

Early one morning, shortly after the sun was up, I walked out of my door to meet Max for one of my airport rides, and there he was actually *talking with Mr. DeMarcantonio*, having just a grand old time discussing something with great animation. They were smiling, gesturing, laughing — and obviously enjoying each other's company. I stayed back a bit so I wouldn't interrupt them. I could now hear them talking about the tomato crop of all things and what a great year it was going to be for home-grown tomatoes.

After several minutes of this friendly banter, Max looked up, noticed me standing there, and said goodbye to Mr. DeMarcantonio.

"Max, what in the world were you guys talking about?" I said as we got into the taxi. "I've never been able to get two words out of him!" My frustration was only thinly disguised.

"Tomatoes, Ed." Max replied.

"Tomatoes! But, how do you even know him?"

"We started talking one morning about our vegetable gardens after he spotted me admiring his. One thing led to another and, on my last trip to pick you up for the airport, I left him some of my tomatoes. Doesn't he have a great garden?"

"Yeah, I guess," I said intrigued by how Max had broken through his wall. "But, I always thought he was just old and wanted to keep to himself."

Max paused a moment.

"Do you really know him to be unapproachable, Ed?" he asked quizzically.

He had me on this one. I said I knew Mr. DeMarcantonio was certainly older than I was, but I had no real basis for saying he was unapproachable. I hadn't ever invested the time in him to be in a position to make that kind of judgment. I guess Max was saying, "Who are you to judge this man who is your neighbor, when you've never made much of an effort to have a genuine conversation with him?"

Somehow, Max had a way of asking questions that delivered his message without being judgmental.

"I hear you, Max," I said. "But, how do I connect with someone who just doesn't seem interested in connecting?"

"Ed, the chances are always pretty good there's common ground somewhere, if you look hard enough to find it."

Come to think of it, Max was all about common ground. You felt it in his taxi — he knew people wanted to feel comfortable, calm, refreshed, and specially treated on their way to wherever they were going, and he had created the perfect environment for this. He knew his customers wanted to talk about themselves, and he had the passion to be interested in and knowledgeable about virtually any topic they might bring up. By providing a friendly, relaxing atmosphere, and by making the effort to connect with what was important to his clients, Max had no trouble at all establishing credible, common ground, even in a vegetable garden.

* * * * *

Fast-forward

I've started my own business providing billing and claims services to physicians and struggling to leverage every ounce of sales skills that I have. At the time, I had no customers, few prospects, and no money. I had been making dozens of sales calls into doctors' offices leading with my products and services and typical sales techniques. This resulted in sales figures that wound up right where you might expect them to be — marginal at best.

Then on one of my calls I visit a doctor's office in the basement of a row home in an economically challenged neighborhood. As I enter, I need to duck my head down some to avoid hitting it on the doorway overhead.

While spending a few minutes in the small, wood-paneled waiting room, I noticed several books about walking with the doctor's name on the cover of each one. This guy really seemed to believe in walking for your health and was not very shy about getting that message out to his patients. I was a runner so the thought of walking versus running was interesting.

Eventually, the nurse escorts me to one of the examining rooms where I wait for the doctor. The doctor enters, does not look up, but asks, "What are your symptoms?"

I clear my throat and say that I'm not a patient but I'm here to see him about his accounts receivable.

He takes my card, glances at it and says, "Mr. Wallace, you have sixty seconds, and you have just used fifteen."

At this point all of the sales training you have goes out the window and instincts need to kick in. After what was likely the longest five-second pause of my life, I took a deep breath and replied, "Doctor I realize that you're very busy, but I can't possibly do justice to explaining my services in that amount of time. Could I ask you a question, though?"

"Shoot," he says.

"In your waiting area, I noticed that you've authored several books on walking. I'm a runner and would love to know why you believe walking is better."

I realize I'm already passed the sixty-second deadline, but what do I have to lose?

The doc's face brightens up.

"I'll tell you why walking is better," he says. "Do you ever notice the faces of people who are running?"

I responded, "They look contorted."

"Exactly. Now, how do the people walking look to you?" he asked.

I got the point. He not only answers my question, but he goes on for thirty minutes about why I should start walking and why he's so passionate about it. I learn that everyone calls him Dr. Fred.

Dr. Fred's office manager is doing her job and has by now tapped on the door three times, but the doc is on a roll and waves her away again. He talks some more about his latest book. Finally, he pauses, looks at me and says, "What were you here to see me about again?"

I explain that my services could possibly help him with his accounts receivable.

He says, "Make an appointment to see Jane, my office manager. And here, take this and start walking tomorrow!" and he hands me one of his books.

During the next few weeks in working with Jane, I discover that Dr. Fred has the largest Blue Cross practice in the entire area, despite his humble office environment, seeing close to ninety patients per day.

While I did gain a few customers with the other sales strategies mentioned earlier, my approach with Dr. Fred lead to him becoming one of my largest accounts and — with full credit to Max — *one of my best friends.*

If I had to attribute the sudden turnaround in that first conversation with Dr. Fred to something, I would attribute it to watching Max and Mr. DeMarcantonio talk about tomatoes. That day, Max helped me realize to always relate to people at a sincere, personal level, by making the effort to find the common ground even if you only have 60 seconds!

Finding common ground is your first opportunity to establish credibility in your business relationships and a satisfying aspect of turning fares into friends.

CHAPTER THREE

No Cutting in Line

On one of my morning rides with Max, I asked him if he also picked up any friends at the airport after he dropped me off — in order to maximize his income, pardon the pun.

"Hey Max," I said, "Seems like a waste of time just driving down here with me and not driving back with a fare."

"Well, Ed," (Whenever Max said, 'Well, Ed,' I knew he was going to deliver some counsel.) "I have an opportunity to do that every time I drop my friends off here." Then his voice kind of trailed off. "I actually did it once when I was first getting started — dropped off a friend and went right around to Arrivals and picked up the next person in line."

"Wow, that really must have been a profitable trip for you, Max," I said.

"Not really, Ed," he said, sounding more serious than I expected.

"Why?" I asked.

"Well, what time is your flight?" he asked. We had just entered the airport complex.

I said that I had another ninety minutes.

"Can you stay with me for a few more minutes? I want to show you something."

"Sure," I said, "Where are we headed?"

Max circled around to an outlying lot near the Arrivals section of the airport.

"Ed, do you see that parking lot, with all of the yellow taxi's lined up?"

"Sure. Man, there are a lot of taxis over there!"

"Yes, and you know what else, Ed? Some of them have been there for hours," he sighed.

"Wow," I said, "They need to find a way to avoid that line."

Max paused. He knew I was still not getting it. Then he tried again.

"Ed, most of those guys are immigrants who have no education, they come to this country, somehow find money to lease a taxi, work from dawn to midnight, never see their families, and spend a great deal of their time in that line. The unwritten rule is that if you want an arrival fare, you wait in that line."

"So," I said, "one day, without knowing all of this, you picked up a fare and cut some other guy out of a fare to the suburbs." I was finally catching on.

"Yes Ed, and to this day I regret it and I won't do it again."

"Oh come on Max, it was only one fare," I said, attempting to rationalize for him.

"Yes it was only one fare, but I didn't play by the rules. Who knows, maybe that next driver in line only picked up a short, local fare for all of the time he spent waiting — because I cut in line and took the larger suburban fare. Someday, I hope the airport will regulate the process better. But, whether they ever do or not, I need to do my best to abide by the unwritten rules, the ethics of my profession."

My experience with Max and the taxi line was very compelling. After reflecting on his integrity over cutting in line at the airport, I realized how private the quality of integrity can be. It's really something for our friends to say, "She has integrity", but even more powerful for us as individuals to live it without any acknowledgement. The airport taxi situation at that time was wide open for abuse without any accountability, yet Max lived his integrity in the face of no real consequences other than of course, his own requirement to sleep at night.

* * * * *

Here's an example of how this played out for me

While I was working at a technology company, I was asked to develop a program to work with key influencers in our market. Corporate America was in the middle of its Y2K anxiety, spending billions on enterprise-wide application software and consulting to make sure everything would work when the clock ticked to 12:00

AM on January 1, 2000.

Our company was doing well by partnering with the key software vendors in our industry. However, we discovered a gap in our strategy around the Big Six accounting firms. (As you probably know, today they are down to the Big Four due to consolidation and Arthur Andersen's troubles.) We learned that these firms often influenced their clients' software purchasing decisions, particularly in our area of specialty. We realized that though our company had a good reputation, our salespeople didn't have much personal connection to any of the Big Six partners and managers who worked closely with our prospects and customers.

I began thinking about how we could work with these key influencers since our CEO was very committed to partnering to help deliver everything our customers needed. Armed with nothing but his support and my own blind gumption, I set out to meet the key national partners at each firm.

Getting in the door for a meeting with each partner turned out to be surprisingly easy – these are not easy contacts to establish – and should have been my first clue that something was not right. After the initial niceties, each Big 6 partner immediately confronted me with, "Why would we work closely with you, since you compete with us?" In the first meeting or two, I was truly caught off-guard by their view of our company as a serious competitor. We had always viewed these firms as potential partners, and both a source of referrals for us and place to refer our customers for consulting.

I realized we had a big integrity issue; apparently, they were still harboring bad feelings over our company's attempt several years earlier to get into consulting. This was our own "cutting in line" issue. It took a lot of reassurance from our CEO and me to convince them that we were no longer interested in this area, and that it was worth their time to even pursue a more collaborative partnership.

It took many months of meetings, calls, and some key social time together to help these firms understand our true intentions, rebuild trust, and to prove to them that we were viable partners.

At last we were on a roll, working with each firm on the best way to partner with us, so their professionals would become expert and certified on our software — leading to potential consulting opportunities for them and positive buying decision influence for our company.

Life was great, until they started talking to Legal. Now, I have some great friends who are attorneys, so this is no slight to them, but even they would agree that legal departments can really slow down a process.

Apparently, what we were proposing amounted to partnerships and their whole structure and culture was based on being a partnership. They didn't partner with anyone, rather they kept everything proprietary, and if they didn't possess a competency they either built it or went out and bought it.

Time to get creative.

I suggested to our CEO that since we had rebuilt trust, that we should use this renewed quality to everyone's benefit and do business with these firms on a simple handshake. No contracts, no formal agreements.

I went on to explain that it could take years just to reach formal agreement on something as simple as an engagement letter. By that time, we would have missed the Y2K opportunity. I said we had pretty much defined the program, built it so each firm could have its own identity, and I felt my relationships with the partners were on solid ground. He said, "Why not!"

With another round of meetings to present our radical proposal (during which I had to pick a couple of Big Six partners up off the floor), I assured them that our CEO and I would personally stand behind this kind of arrangement putting our reputations in the industry on the line.

Miraculously, each firm agreed to our concept.

A parallel challenge you will face when developing business partnerships is working with your internal operational folks to make the partnership work. The last thing that well-oiled finance, customer service, sales, IT, and education groups need is for some business development person to approach them with a partnership such as this and disrupt their protocols, controls, and established routines.

We were fortunate in this case to have collaborated with each of these key groups throughout the process so when it came time to turn the switch on with the Big 6, everything went very smoothly. It did not hurt of course that outstanding business relationships were forged with these folks over the years resulting in support for such a challenging project.

After three years in the program, our company earned significant referral revenue annually and the Big Six consulting practices were each generating several times that amount in revenues from working with our products.

To top it off, we were even able to get them all to come together for an annual conference to collaborate on common issues — something previously unheard of in their fiercely competitive environment.

How did this happen?

Certainly, this accomplishment required a lot of one-on-one time talking with the national partners, and lots of time meeting with various Big Six practice offices. It took constant availability to help with questions and conflicts, and consistency of judgment when judgment calls were needed. And it required some political savvy to navigate the process, with each firm believing it was the best and competing with the others at every turn.

But behind all that, what really made it possible was our determination to build an environment of fairness, ethics, and trust. We wanted to create an atmosphere of integrity in these relationships where they could trust us as well as each other, and concentrate on the potential for expanding the size of the pie for all versus the usual concept of everyone fighting for the biggest piece of a limited pie.

In other words, even the big boys will do business on a handshake if they trust you not to cut in line.

Chapter Four

The Power of "I Don't Know"

After many rides together, Max began to realize that I was taking a lot of the things he was saying pretty seriously. I was relatively young and impressionable, so one day Max turned to me and said, "Ed, you know I really enjoy our conversations. But I hope you're making your own careful decisions on the matters we discuss, because I would feel really awful if something didn't work out for you because you took some comment I made too seriously."

At that point I needed to come clean with Max and admit that I was seeing him, to some degree, as a father figure. He had such a caring way; he listened to me and guided me. I explained that my own father had passed away recently and that getting to know Max had gone a long way toward filling the hole that remained in my life.

"Max," I said, "I don't mean to put you on the spot, but your advice has been important to me."

"It's OK, Ed." he said. "Let's make a deal. From here on in, I'll keep that in mind and maybe I can be more of a mentor to you, since a mentor helps you find your own truth rather than imposing his truth on you. How's that work for you?"

Now, this was well before mentoring became a mainstream approach in the fields of leadership and management. I had hardly ever heard the term, except maybe in an old Kung Fu episode. Yet Max, my friendly taxi driver, was offering to be one to me.

Next, Max had a revelation or two of his own to share with me in return. He said that I was filling a need for him as well.

"You know I enjoy my time with all my friends, but when you and I get together the entire trip is different. You listen to what I have to say! You've become a kind of student of my life experiences and that means a lot. Plus, I really enjoy your company."

Then he paused a while and started to speak again. He told me that before he drove a taxi, he had been an executive for a large company, at one point accepting an important assignment to work in the Middle East in the late 1970s. Unfortunately, his assignment also coincided with the Iran hostage crisis in 1979 — in which 66 American diplomats and civilians were taken captive in the U.S. Embassy — a situation that dragged on for fourteen months, bedeviled the Carter administration and cast a long shadow over U.S. foreign affairs. It had been an extremely challenging and dangerous time to be an American working in the Middle East.

By that time Max had learned a variety of strategies for developing friends and as well as the protocols for survival, for communication, looking out for others in the community, and for managing the day-to-day logistics of living and working under hostile conditions. He had to become an expert, not only in his original field of business, but in the cultural, political and economic realities that dominated every aspect of life there at that time.

But, at some point, once the crisis was resolved he came to a decision that he'd had enough — of the politics, the pressure, the danger, stress and anxiety. He thought hard and deeply about what was important in his life, and he began to reorganize his priorities. He and his family moved back to the United States. He desired to live a simple life of service to people, taking the lessons he had learned about human nature, relationships and life, applying and sharing these freely in a helpful way. This was the point at which he purchased a taxi and set up his business providing rides, wisdom and friendship.

Through our friendship, Max told me he had found not only another "friend", not only pleasant companionship, but someone who understood his life work and to whom he could, in effect, authentically share it with, in the hopes it would continue to benefit others in some small way.

Now I knew some essential things about Max that I hadn't known before, and he knew some essential things about me that he hadn't known before. This put our relationship on a much more authentic basis. By being willing to "come clean" and simply be who we were at that time, we were better able to appreciate and help each other in ways that made a difference.

* * * * *

Being True to Yourself

This has been a key lesson for me in my life and business. Too often, we put a lot of energy into keeping up a façade in our business relationships — an appearance of strength, expertise, influence or success — for fear that others will see us as weak or vulnerable. To the contrary, I've found that when I'm comfortable just being who I am — to be authentically me, without embellishment or bragging — people tend to believe and respect me, and we make more progress in whatever project stands before us.

Often, the willingness to be your unvarnished self will result in the words, "I don't know." I learned that a big turning point in a career is to be able to admit this to yourself and others. No longer needing to "fake it until you make it" as the saying goes. To Max, these three words were like magic. He thought one of the hardest things for business people, especially as they are trying to move up the ladder, is to admit openly that they don't have all the answers. But, saying "I don't know" can open the doors to a healthy discussion about possible solutions and resources that could lead to an answer. The fact that the individual may be admitting that he or she isn't the ultimate source of wisdom on the matter in question is not relevant; what is relevant is that everyone is able to focus on the need itself and how to meet it most effectively, together. Intellectual honesty is rare air these days.

On this point, I witnessed an amazing phenomenon in my son's fourth grade class during Observation Day. The teacher was going over some math problems, and they were challenging — at least to me. Yet, the kids were absolutely fearless in their attempts to answer each question. They had no anxiety over possible failure or what the others thought of them — only enthusiasm to attempt the challenge. They embraced Max's magic words, I don't know, and relished the task of finding the right answer.

We're often so guarded in our business relationships, so afraid to show our real selves. Think about all the meetings you've been in where an executive is droning on with a presentation — (Picture actor Ben Stein with his dry delivery in front of a meeting room) — and everyone in the room is just following the words on each slide, mentally glazing over and not willing to engage in any real discussion. I believe that it is because we're afraid of the dynamics, the politics of the people in the room, afraid of what they would think of us, or what might happen to our job if we said something that implied we didn't totally comprehend everything being presented.

I recall a story that Max shared about a very successful, retired CEO who launched a cottage industry out of her home and wound up being an industry giant. She was one of his regular riders and once shared with him an experience about a talk she was giving to a small group of former colleagues on a topic that she had basically built her reputation on. When asked what seemed to be a very fundamental question, she responded, "You know, I never thought of it that way!" The room went silent because everyone had a perspective on the topic yet the expert was freely admitting that she did not know. Guess what happened? Her former colleagues recognized and were comfortable responding to her authenticity. They made the issue a rallying point of common ground resulting in a spirit of "we'll work this out together". Committees were formed and a whole new strategy emerged that basically reinvented the previous work of the CEO. The corporation achieved significant growth again as a result of the strategy, people were promoted, and new jobs were created.

Finally, on a much smaller scale, I know from my own experience that being authentic and true to yourself, pays off. Recently, I was visiting one of my regular client companies, a large, very well-known service firm. They were telling me about a problem they had with employee satisfaction. They wanted me to help them put together a workshop for their employees. I said frankly that my focus did not extend to that area, and I wasn't sure I knew how to do it. Without missing a beat, my client said, "You may not know how to do it, but I know you and you will figure it out. You've always managed to figure things out in the other work we've done together and I know we'll work together to figure this out, too."

My willingness to be authentic with my client about my capabilities in the face of turning away business did not risk anything; it only confirmed their comfort with me and opened the way for a new and interesting project which ultimately succeeded.

Sometimes just saying the magic, authentic words, 'I don't know,' can result in amazing things!

CHAPTER FIVE

Remember 168 and Bellybuttons

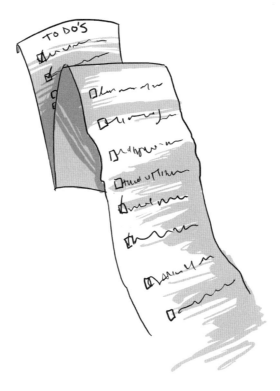

I mentioned earlier that most of this book would be devoted to exploring how to have quality in your relationships. Note the word "most." This chapter is in some ways, an exception. It's about the importance of time. The reason I'm including it is that the simple lesson Max taught me about time has a lot to do with making it possible to *have* these relationships that I'm talking about. And his lesson *is* simple; but, I figured if I'm distracted enough to need a simple lesson like this, you may be too.

On yet another trip to the airport, I was a bit detached and Max commented, "Seems like you're pretty busy today, Ed?"

"Oh, sorry Max, I've got proposals, memos, expense reports — and that's not the half of it. I just can't keep up!" I sighed.

"That's got to be very frustrating. Seems like you're caught in a vicious cycle," he said.

"Right, and that cycle seems endless. Any suggestions?"

Max knew he was on the spot again, but without changing his vocal inflection, he asked, "Do you know anything about the number 168, Ed?"

"168, 168? What's that all about?" I asked.

"Well, think about it," he said. "What could it represent?"

"Max, I'm drowning here, and you're playing paint by numbers with me! Can you give me a clue?" I asked frantically.

"Okay. We all have as much in common with the number 168 as we do with having a bellybutton." Max continued.

168 and bellybuttons, now I'm really lost.

"Think Ed, think about *time* Ed. That's what you're asking about. Think!" he asked.

"Time is days, weeks, minutes, hours…." I mulled.

"Hours! Now you're getting warm," he cheered.

"Hours? There are 24 hours in a day and I don't have enough of them."

"OK, and how many hours are there in a week?"

Uh,…I am now multiplying 7 times 24 in my head and guess what? It comes out to 168!

"Max, you rascal, you could have just told me that right off the bat!" I responded.

"You know Ed, then it may have been too easy and you might not have recognized the value in knowing that number." He mused.

"I still don't see the value," I said. "We all have bellybuttons and we all have 168 hours in a week. So what?"

"Precisely, we all have the same amount of time. We also have a great deal of freedom in the ways that we choose to use it. Ed, how do you think the leaders of all the big corporations got to where they are? How did they find the time to do everything that had to be done to make a living, develop new skills, develop relationships, advance their careers and lead these global businesses?"

I proudly confessed, *"I don't know!"*

"Well Ed, I'll tell you," he started "they have the same amount of time in the day as you and me, but they make a choice on how to spend their time because it is what they want to do, what they believe in. I made a choice to drive a taxi, but in my own way because I wanted to spend my time in service to my friends. You know, if you like what you're doing, you'll never work another day in your life."

He continued, "You appear to have chosen to try to squeeze a lot of busy activity into your time. Ever wonder what that activity is producing?"

I could not say anything else at that moment because we arrived at the airport.

"What airline today, Ed?"

"USAir, thanks," I said.

With that, I had to leave Max's lesson on time, but I had a lot to reflect on during my flight.

* * * * *

Fast Forward

I took a corporate sales position with a major corporation. I had a pretty decent first year, but part way into the second year my boss stopped by my office one day and sat down. Now, Jim was not a hard-driving sales manager, more of a Father Flannigan counselor type. He asked how I thought things were going. This was his way of opening a conversation about how my performance was slipping, without saying, "Ed, your sales are off." And they were well behind quota.

I answered, "Jim, I keep working harder and harder, but my sales aren't improving. In fact they're getting worse."

"Seems like you need to think about where and how you're focusing your time, Ed," he said.

So, despite my dedication to developing strong personal relationships, friendships that would turn into business relationships, I wasn't paying enough attention to all the little factors that tended to eat away at my time, making it increasingly harder for me to bring those relationships to fruition.

Jim talked for another few minutes, but I kept visualizing the word TIME above his head and remembering Max's comments on time from a few years before. We agreed that I would come back to him with some thinking on this problem and that we'd work together on a plan to improve my performance.

I remembered how simple time seemed when Max discussed it. He had basically reduced it to the ridiculous with the number 168 and bellybuttons, and emphasis on our freedom to use time as we chose.

So, I thought about how sales people spend their time. We look for commonalities with the buyer. We try to differentiate ourselves from the competition. We all prospect, we all have a sales cycle, and we all have a contract to get signed. We all try to make a monthly quota.

Not much there, so I dug deeper on each step in the process. As far as I could see, every step was essential. So, I began looking for a different approach, some way to be different and more effective. I thought about this for weeks. Jim was getting a bit anxious since his boss was getting a bit anxious.

Finally, one night I woke up and said out loud, "That's it, that's it!" Now I knew how Keith Richard of The Rolling Stones must have felt when legend has it that he woke up one night and jotted down the opening chords to the all-time hit song, *Satisfaction*.

Laurie woke up and asked, somewhat bemused, "Now what are you conjuring up?"

"I think I cracked the code," I said.

"Cracked what code?" she asked in a tone that indicated "he's at it again!"

"Honey, please just go back to sleep, I need to go and write this down," I responded.

The words that I wrote down were simply *Timing* and *Process*.

The next day I looked at my prospect list and asked myself the same question about each one: "Will they buy from me on the 24th of the month instead of the 31st?" I thought through all of them and was able to answer Y*es* for about 50% percent of the list.

I realized that I had been caught up in the same cycle that my prospects were caught up in. They needed to make buying decisions at the same time that sales people like me had to close business. It made for a very busy time during that last week of every month. Inevitably, I had to give away value in the crunch and my customers weren't always completing all of their ordering on time either.

So, I sat down with Jim and asked if I could try a strategy that created an internal deadline for me by the 24th of every month rather than the end of the month. He blinked, since he had been at this for many years and had never heard of this one before. Eventually, he OK'd the plan, but just for one quarter and with two conditions (these are nice tips for sales people by the way):

First I had to create two Top Ten Lists of prospects. I think that Jim must have been watching too much David Letterman at the time. To make the first list, I needed to be able to do something for the prospect every day to move them through the sales cycle. If I could not, then they could not be on the first list. The second list was there to catch all of those that I could not work on every day. This seemed fair enough.

The second condition and this is the one that would ultimately make or break my success with this approach was to be authentic enough *to ask each prospect for their help.*

I asked Jim, "Why would I ask for help?"

To this day Jim's answer remains incredibly ironic to me since he never knew Max, but seemed to be coming from the same place.

"Asking for help infers friendship and friends help each other!" he commented.

Jim went on to explain that whether you are in a sales process or any business relationship, asking for help is a very powerful request. It will determine right then and there whether you have built a strong business relationship. Jim knew that this would not only help me qualify my prospects but, that in many cases human nature could work in my favor as well by seeking help from fellow human beings.

So, armed with Jim's techniques and support, I set out to contact each prospect who was close to a buying decision and asked for their help with my idea of closing business earlier each month. Now, everyone was not ready to do this, but many more than the 50% that I expected agreed at least to explore trying to get their contracts signed sooner. This got the process in motion.

After a few months, I was rolling. My orders were coming in by the third week of every month, our production people had more time to get their end-of-month orders processed and customers were receiving their orders sooner. Now, I was able to be out doing what I enjoyed best, prospecting — *building relationships* — while my competitors were still trying to close business. I felt I was always a few days to a week ahead of the pack — a very sweet feeling, indeed.

And guess what? That year, my telesales rep and I had the number one producing territory leading to the Sales Team of the Year award.

Upon reflection, I can trace this success not only to my lesson on time and how best to use this natural resource, but the knowledge of the inherent desire in people to want to help their friends.

Comedian/philosopher Steven Wright once said something like, "Everywhere is within walking distance, if you have the time!"

I felt like - *Everywhere* **was** *within walking distance because I made the time.*

Part I Summary

As I mentioned previously, my hope for you as you read this book is that you will come away with a renewed appreciation for the value of developing outstanding business relationships. In Part 1, I shared my experiences with Max and how they allowed me to apply and benefit from an awareness and use of the following simple concepts for developing outstanding business relationships:

1. Seek common ground

2. Earn trust

3. Be yourself

4. Use time purposefully

* * * * *

Moving forward, Part II of this book will emphasize why developing outstanding business relationships is more important than ever for business and personal success. I'll continue to explain what Max modeled through the use of a unique term, Relational Capital, and how you can determine whether you have any of it. Next, I'll share the experiences of three successful business partners who live this stuff everyday and finally, close with more about my friend Max.

PART II

I Call it Relational Capital

CHAPTER SIX

The Importance of Relational Capital

Today's business leaders face incredible challenges. They participate on teams, manage functional groups, and basically do their best to help fellow employees manage the pressures of their jobs. The Internet and pace of communications puts business leaders on call 24/7 with seemingly little time for anything but meeting the bottom line.

On that point, the *Harvard Business Review* recently noted that there are two main factors colliding with traditional management process and structure in the 21st Century business environment:

1. The movement toward more collaborative management structures;

2. The urgency of work due to the pace of technology.

As recently as a couple of decades ago, traditional management structure was still largely intact, with the familiar hallmarks of vertical, command-and-control decision making that proceeded slowly within departmental silos.

With the tsunami of technological change occurring in the 1980s and 1990s — including the process improvements inherent in enterprise-wide systems like SAP and Oracle, and tools like Lotus Notes — traditional management has been widely replaced by flattened, matrix-style organizations. These organizations are characterized by collaboration and virtual teaming with distributed leadership and, at times, lack of clarity on who is actually making the decisions.

The flow of work, which once could bog down and be traced to a single, isolated individual or department, is now broadly influenced by large numbers of project participants, whose collective stake in project outcomes creates a relentless sense of urgency to drive completion of the tasks at hand.

The information overload and the breathtaking pace of today's work environment have left many business leaders struggling just to keep up, let alone to manage effectively.

Consequently, at an individual level, business relationships have suffered significantly; they're often reduced to a series of short-term transactions between BlackBerry® devices, not people! Suddenly, checking items off our to-do lists is mistaken for actual performance.

I can't tell you how many times that I emailed the person in the office right next door to me! An opportunity to handle something in person was handled electronically, simply due to the number of emails that I had to dispense with.

At other times, I've left work on a Friday feeling like I added value to my company, based solely on the fact that I had emptied this same email inbox!

However, two constants remain through all of these 21st Century dynamics:

1. Business is still driven by people and relationships, not tasks or project plans.

2. People have not changed in regard to their need for human interaction and outstanding business relationships.

As I mentioned, Part I of this book was intended to help you experience just how Max turned 'fares to friends.' However, since my years riding with Max I've struggled to define in business terms his abstract wisdom for developing outstanding business relationships. As I pressed on, I learned some interesting facts:

Over half the market value of Fortune 500 companies today is contributed by intangible assets.

- These intangible assets include intellectual property, brands, corporate reputation, employees, acquired goodwill and customer relationships
- These intangible assets are also critical sources of income, referrals, repeat business, financial growth and competitive differentiation

In fact, the intangible assets comprised of customer, employee and supplier relationships are sometimes referred to as relational capital. The relational capital of companies is so important and valuable that some investors will pay a large premium above book value to own shares of these companies.

The same perception of value can be applied to people when calculating and growing their personal net worth in life and business.

Your intangible assets include your knowledge and skills, educational background, reputation and your personal and professional relationships.

Your intangible assets:
- Provide access to business and career opportunities that generate income
- Attract people and business opportunities to you

- Generate referrals and repeat business
- Create a network of people that can offer help and resources to you
- Make your life and career more enjoyable

These intangible assets can be viewed as your *personal* Relational Capital. Therefore, for the balance of this book, I will be using the term **Relational Capital** to describe the value and the power of investing in business relationships on which the success of any career is ultimately based.

Here's my definition:

> ### Relational Capital
>
> The value created by people in a business relationship; the most important element in a business relationship.

Now, let's connect the idea of Relational Capital to the three essential qualities mentioned in Part 1, that go into building outstanding business relationships — **credibility, integrity, and authenticity**.

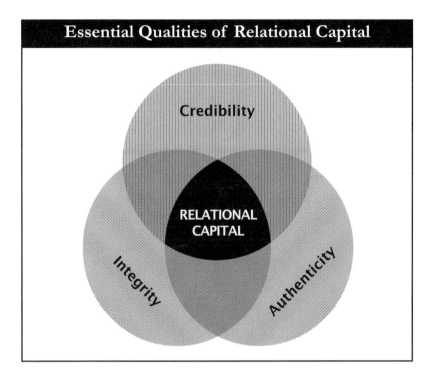

Essential Qualities of Relational Capital

These are the essential qualities — the distinctive DNA that converges to create high levels of Relational Capital in business relationships.

Essentially, *How people know and regard you!*

Here's a more detailed explanation of these essential qualities of Relational Capital:

Credibility

The American Heritage Dictionary defines credibility as "The quality, capability, or power to elicit belief."

Everything about Max created credibility for me — his demeanor, enthusiasm, knowledge, and his taxi. I believed he was committed to being in service to my travel needs and that he was more than capable of delivering on that commitment.

In my case, I had zero credibility with Mr. DeMarcantonio because all I ever invested was a hello. However, when my opportunity came to develop credibility with Dr. Fred, instead of just pushing a sale, I took time to become personally interested in an unusual aspect of his expertise — walking and writing books about walking. He realized that my interest was sincere and consequently, that I was the kind of person with whom he would like to do business.

Integrity

Dictionary.com defines integrity as, "adherence to moral and ethical principles; soundness of moral character; honesty."

Max's integrity was evident from the start of our friendship. Fairness, honesty and ethics were fundamental values to him, seen in how he treated his clients, charged for his services, how he sadly turned away business when he knew he couldn't deliver on additional commitments and how he refused to cut in line in front of his fellow cabbies.

In my efforts with the Big 6, I first needed to overcome an integrity issue over our firm competing with them before I could eventually do business with them on a handshake.

Authenticity

The American Heritage Dictionary defines authenticity as "The quality or condition of being authentic, trustworthy, or genuine."

My friendship with Max took on deeper dimensions after we became more authentic with each other, true to our own spirit and character and open about our backgrounds, circumstances and motivations. I learned a lesson about authenticity in being willing to tell clients *"I don't know"* and trusting that I would not lose anything by being myself.

* * * * *

Chapter Summary

1. The focus on building outstanding business relationships is more critical today than ever before due to the move toward collaborative management structures and the pace and impact of technological change.

2. Relational Capital is the value created by people in a business relationship; the most important element in a business relationship.

3. The essential qualities of credibility, integrity, and authenticity converge to form Relational Capital in business relationships.

CHAPTER SEVEN

Relational Capital Value Creation

Relational Capital is created and developed through the convergence of the essential qualities of credibility, integrity, and authenticity as well as the purposeful use of time that we learned from Max. In addition, each of these qualities can be thought of as an abstract equivalent of basic financial principles. For example:

- Open Relational Capital "accounts" with others by <u>establishing common ground</u> with them

- Secure and protect each account by demonstrating <u>integrity and trustworthiness</u>

- Make investments in each account through the <u>purposeful use of time</u> with people

- Grow the value of each account by <u>offering authentic help and assistance</u>

- Generate significant returns on Relational Capital through <u>appropriate requests for help</u>

Relational Capital Gains

Developing outstanding business relationships is a multi-dimensional process that evolves as the essential qualities of credibility, integrity, and authenticity become stronger and begin to converge in a business relationship. This convergence occurs all through the process and results in what I call, **Relational Capital Gains** — a dynamic increase in reserves of trust and goodwill. Relational Capital Gains lead to long-term sustainable business relationships and guess what else? Friendships! (let's not forget about turning fares into friends)

The following model depicts the examples from the previous page and demonstrates how Relational Capital Gains increase in intensity over time, leading to outstanding business relationships.

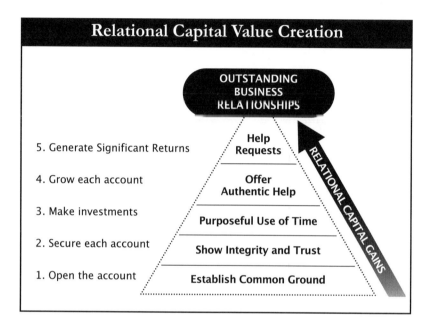

Whether you choose to view Relational Capital as a practical or abstract metric, it is extremely meaningful in the experience of those who have it. Here's why:

- High value relationships are better equipped to weather inevitable business downturns and other uncontrollable factors

- Relational Capital transforms a business environment from a focus on transactions and tactical accomplishment to a focus on the value each party brings to the relationship

- Relational Capital helps people transcend the automatic sense of urgency and panic that permeates much of today's work world because both parties are operating on a higher plane, working as friends, and better able to identify real priorities and achieve real productivity for each other. Remember, 'friends help each other!'

Relational Capital Checklist

As in the Relational Capital Value Creation model, you will likely always have some percentage of contacts with whom you have outstanding Relational Capital and others that you will really need to work harder to improve your Relational Capital.

Here is an informal, partial list of common indicators that you are generally building significant Relational Capital with your contacts and colleagues. You will have others you could add to the list. The more of these you can identify as being present in your business relationships, the more likely it is that you are experiencing the benefits of Relational Capital:

- ☑ You are able to ask for help from colleagues and customers.

- ☑ People from all levels in your organization take you into their confidence and seek your help and input.

- ☑ Customers share confidences with you and invite you into their planning processes.

- ☑ Your decisions that turn into mistakes are viewed as

opportunities rather than admonishments.

☑ Open and honest conversations with your manager do not lead to career risk.

☑ You are confident that a buying decision for a higher price is the right one due to your relationship with the vendor.

☑ You continue to be a valued reference for people as they move through their own career opportunities.

☑ You view negative input from your customers as an opportunity to strengthen the relationship.

☑ You are comfortable referring business that you cannot effectively provide.

☑ You are invited to join high profile projects.

☐ Add your own:

_____

_____

_____

_____

How do we learn to get it?

So now that we have defined and analyzed Relational Capital how do we really learn to get it like Max got it? How do we get to a place where we recognize the value of Relational Capital — where we focus on the people in the business relationship and their long-term objectives, not just the immediate, tangible products generated by our work? How do we break through the new business environment processes and methodologies to get to real business relationships? How do we come to really understand the value of "How people know and regard us?"

One way is to go back to basics and focus on the essential qualities of Relational Capital: credibility, integrity, and authenticity. However, when I set out to write this book and to share my experiences, I wasn't sure how to develop these qualities. We already possess them, we just need to learn to appreciate and value them more.

One answer is by "re-appreciating" these qualities that constitute outstanding business relationships and by remembering that most real accomplishments — whether it's the sale of a product or service or the advancement of a career — involve human beings listening to, understanding and helping one another in the ways that look a lot like friendship.

Charles Schultz, the creator of the beloved *Peanuts* cartoon characters, once said something like — "while people may or may not long remember who won what award, contest or prize or set which world record — they will always remember someone who has listened to them, appreciated or helped them in solving a problem or overcoming an obstacle."

Chapter Summary

1. Relational Capital is created and developed through the convergence of the essential qualities of credibility, integrity, and authenticity along with the purposeful use of time.

2. Each of these qualities can be thought of as the abstract equivalent of basic financial principles:

   - Open Relational Capital "accounts" with others by establishing common ground with them

   - Secure and protect each account by demonstrating integrity and trustworthiness

   - Make investments in each account through the purposeful use of time with people

   - Grow the value of each account by offering authentic help and assistance

3. Developing outstanding business relationships is a multidimensional process that evolves as the essential qualities grow stronger and converge in a business relationship to generate Relational Capital Gains.

CHAPTER EIGHT

Relational Capital Lite

today's
Sound Bites

I spoke earlier in this book of work urgency and how everything happens instantaneously and electronically these days. This brings up another term I like to use: **Sound Bites.** We've all heard the term a thousand times: it's what they call the snappy statements that politicians make in front of cameras and microphones to convey in a few seconds their position on a public issue, their take on recent events or their opinion of something the opposition has just said or done.

When I use the term Sound Bites in talking about Relational Capital development, I'm talking about the labels and one-liners that business people formulate about each other. *Rising star; Rookie; Old guard; Super salesperson; Out of his/her league; Team player; Threat; Leader.*

When you walk into a meeting, Sound Bites describing you replay automatically in people's minds. These reinforce how they identify you and reflect your Relational Capital with them.

Let's imagine Max's Relational Capital Sound Bites…

1. Kind, welcoming
2. Truly interested in my life and well being
3. Good business person

With the increased need to work collaboratively both within and outside organizations, your Relational Capital can certainly impact your career. Here's some data from a CEO Resources survey to support this point.

In large companies:

- 40% of CEOs fail within their first 18 months on the job
- 46% of newly hired employees also fail within a similar time frame
- 82% of hiring managers overlook interpersonal skills

In my opinion, a common thread in these statistics is that a lot of people are focusing on "hard skills" and inadvertently ignoring or marginalizing the importance of Relational Capital skills. Hiring at all levels is being based on traditional procedures — how the candidate looks on paper, how well they did in an interview and maybe checking out a reference or two. They are finding out after it's too late that what really matters is how people perceive you in an actual business relationship.

So by now I hope that you're asking yourself, How do I find out about my Relational Capital?

On one hand, the use of an assessment tool, commonly called 360 feedback (360), could help to give you a lot of insights into your Relational Capital. These assessments produce a profile of an individual's relationships with others — peers, direct reports, managers, clients, vendors, etc. — based on confidential responses to survey questions about the individual's skills, interpersonal style, effectiveness, ethics, character and so forth. These tools help leaders get a more comprehensive picture of how others perceive them, how effective their management style is and what steps they might take to improve.

Many leaders, however, will not have the option or be inclined to do a comprehensive 360 feedback evaluation of their skills and relationships with others. This is due to time and cost factors, anxiety over what might be learned, or to the practical realities of their role within an organization or status as an independent contractor.

So, I would like to offer a somewhat less ambitious and less formal way to achieve some of the same results. I believe that much of what we need to know can be figured out by being honest with ourselves and by generally paying attention to what's going on around us.

With that in mind, I present to you the Relational Capital (RC) Lite Assessment. I am calling it Lite, because it simply provides a little guidance and gives some structure and focus to your thought processes around your Relational Capital.

The RC Lite Assessment consists of two parts:
- How I Know and Regard Others, and
- How I See Myself

Each part includes an opportunity to assess the essential Relational Capital qualities of **credibility**, **integrity**, and **authenticity**.

My theory goes like this: If I work through the mechanics of how I know and regard others, then this will give me insights on how others operate when forming their perceptions of me. And then if I am authentic and open about how I see myself and why, I can understand whether I have Relational Capital with my colleagues and how I might go about improving it. In short, sometimes looking through a window at others can help us with seeing ourselves in a mirror.

Relational Capital Lite Assessment

Part I: How I Know and Regard Others

Think of three people with whom you have regular business dealings. At least one of them should be someone you have somewhat mixed feelings about. I've filled in the following worksheet as an example, but you can get blank copies at www.farestofriends.com.

1. Relationship I want to understand better:

   Mike from Accounting

2. **Sound Bites: How do I see this person?**
   Try to find a leadership/interpersonal strength as well as any blind spots; remember, keep it short!

   Nice person; great technical skills; lacks leadership drive

3. **RCI (Relational Capital Index):**
   Score your relationship from 1 to 3 points based on the Sound Bites, where 1 = low, 2 = medium, and 3 = high.

Quality		Score
Credibility:	I find this person to be "believable."	*1*
	This person inspires confidence in me with his/her "knowledge and capabilities."	*1*
Integrity:	In my eyes they are "trustworthy" and have "high ethics."	*3*
	They are "fair" in their dealings with me.	*2*
Authenticity:	This person is "genuine" and "direct."	*2*
	This person is "clear" and open in their communications.	*2*
	RCI TOTAL:	*11*

4. RCI Interpretation:

Circle the range that corresponds with the RCI total from step three. Provide a brief rationale for the rating.

Your RCI Total	Your Rationale
14-18: This person has excellent Relational Capital with me.	
9-13: This person has good Relational Capital with me, but needs to strengthen one area.	*Mike is not aware that he is perceived as just wanting to do his accounting job, yet as he grows in his role it calls for more team leadership and participation.*
4-8: This person has weak Relational Capital with me; needs to focus on weakest areas immediately.	
0-3: This person has NO Relational Capital with me – needs to assess whether due to their lack of knowing me – or some other aspect of our experiences.	

Relational Capital Lite Assessment

Part II: How I See Myself

Now that you are warmed up using the RC Lite Assessment for others, my hope is that you will realize that your colleagues have Sound Bites on you as well. So, this part is about being authentic in relation to your own leadership and interpersonal strengths and blind spots.

Complete the RC Lite Assessment for how you see yourself:

1. **Sound Bites: How do I see myself?**
   Try to find a leadership/interpersonal strength as well as any blind spots; remember, keep it short!

2. **RCI (Relational Capital Index):**
   Score yourself from 1 to 3 points based on your Sound Bites, where 1 = low, 2 = medium, and 3 = high.

Quality		Score
Credibility:	People find me to be "believable."	
	I inspire confidence in others with my "knowledge and capabilities."	
Integrity:	In others' eyes, I am "trustworthy" and have "high ethics."	
	Others would say I am "fair" in my dealings with them.	
Authenticity:	People believe I am "genuine" and "direct."	
	Others would say I am "transparent" and open in my communication.	
	RCI TOTAL:	

3. **RCI Interpretation:**
   Circle the range that corresponds with the RCI total from step three. Provide a brief rationale for the rating.

Your RCI Total	Your Rationale
14-18: I have excellent Relational Capital with my colleagues.	
9-13: I have good Relational Capital, but need to strengthen one area.	
4-8: I have weak Relational Capital in many areas; need to focus on the weakest areas immediately.	
0-3: I have NO Relational Capital with my colleagues; need to assess whether due to their lack of knowing me — or some other aspect of our experiences.	

4. **Next Steps**
   Take a few minutes to reflect on the rationale for your RCI score above. Your challenge now is to find out whether the way you see yourself is accurate and then to begin working on what you discover. A 360 assessment is a logical formal step, but in the meantime, think about some steps you can take immediately to encourage positive Sound Bites from your colleagues and raise your RCI.

1. _____

2. _____

3. _____

Chapter Summary

1. We all have levels of Relational Capital — "How people know and regard us."

2. The Relational Capital Lite Assessment will give you a fresh perspective on your own levels of Relational Capital and how you might go about working on some of your current business relationships.

3. Get back to basics by remembering that nothing takes the place of solid reserves of credibility, integrity, and authenticity.

CHAPTER NINE

Bernie, Jeff, and Phil

To this point in Part II, I have defined Relational Capital, explained the value it brings to business relationships and some ways to understand whether you have it.

Now, it seems appropriate to share an outstanding example of some people who instinctively understand the concepts of Relational Capital development and practice them daily in their business. In thinking about this, it took me all of about ten seconds to decide I wanted to introduce you to Bernie, Jeff, and Phil — my friends at 44 Financial. This boutique commercial mortgage company is a microcosm of why Relational Capital investment works in developing outstanding business relationships.

In a stately but unremarkable old building situated near Philadelphia's historic Antique Row neighborhood, 44 Financial is owned by three native Philly guys. Any images you might have in your mind about mortgage companies or what mortgage offices usually look like do not apply to 44 Financial.

There is no sign identifying their business anywhere on the building — only those of the other tenants on the lower floors. Inside the small vestibule over the mailboxes, a tiny label indicates one of the intercom buttons as belonging to 44 Financial. After you ring, a woman's voice greets you and she quickly buzzes the main door open to a classic old elevator complete with a gated steel door that you open and close manually.

Arriving on the fourth floor, you find no impressive lobby with high-end furniture or thick carpets. Instead, you find a pale yellow hallway leading to a series of offices. There is no formality or requirement to be announced, you simply walk down the hallway to one of my friends' offices.

At any given time, the partners, Bernie, Jeff, and Phil, might be found in one of the offices swapping stories and laughing uncontrollably with former professional football players, local TV celebrities, or your average business owner — any of whom may be there doing business or just reconnecting with their old friends. In the conference room, one minute there's a closing about to wrap up — people in suits signing papers involving hundreds of thousands of dollars — and the next minute the ties are loosened, ESPN appears on the television, and work collides with laughter and fun.

However, laughter and fun aside, the essential fact about this firm — and the reason it's a perfect example of Relational Capital in action — is that its business is entirely dependent upon referrals, which means it's based totally on the quality of Bernie, Jeff, and Phil's relationships. Their actual customers are what they call the big three: bankers, attorneys and accountants who work regularly with small and medium-sized businesses. Sometimes, these small to medium-sized businesses encounter difficulties — such as credit problems, a lawsuit or impending foreclosure — where standard types of financing aren't available to them, and their banker, lawyer or accountant has to refer them to a specialty firm for help. It's my friends' goal to maintain such good relations with these three groups that the referral they think of first is always 44 Financial.

Phil started the firm in 1987. He liked reading about management and leadership and one of his favorite books was Harvey Mackay's *Swim With The Sharks Without Being Eaten Alive*, which listed sixty-six things you need to know about your client. Phil drew up his own list and arrived at forty-four, including where they were born, where they went to school, the names of their spouses and kids, the kids' ages and so forth. Someone suggested he name his new company

44 Financial and that was that. Phil's philosophy was simple — get to really know your friends. (*The "44" Profile* is included in the Appendix)

Soon, Jeff, an old friend of Phil's, left a job at Westinghouse to help broker loans with the new firm. Bernie, Jeff's uncle, came to them from the commercial real estate business. They felt they all worked well together because their personalities were compatible, they had a similar sense of business ethics and values, and they loved having fun while they worked.

From the start, they knew that knowing the referring client intimately was the key to their success. The hardest part of their business is to get this client to give a referral. This is because when the bank's or attorney's own reputation and relationships are at stake; they need to know that they are sending their customer to a company they fully trust to treat people fairly and honestly, and to solve the problem effectively.

If you ask him about this challenge, Phil says, "In our business, people can exist without us. We have a good service to provide, but there are others providing the same service, so our job is to get the client to think of us and to send us the business because they like the way we treat their customer."

Bernie says it differently reflecting on his earlier days: "Asking someone to send you a customer on trust is like asking them to set you up with a blind date. It has to be someone they have a high regard for. They have to think, 'Who am I going to send on a date with this person? Who can I trust to really come through and not disappoint or embarrass me?' You have to get to that point in developing the relationship."

An important aspect of how they work is that they have a well-developed sense of which one of them would be the most appropriate fit with a given client — in terms of what they have in common, background, roots, etc. Phil may hit it off especially well with certain people and Jeff or Bernie better with others. They are a diverse team and each is a true original; they don't fit any mold for people in their line of work. Bernie, the senior member of the group, is an expert (and tireless) storyteller and can keep a group listening and laughing for hours. Jeff played basketball at Villanova and then also coached at an NCAA Division I basketball program so he connects well with people with a love for sports. Phil is a trained musician — an opera buff and an accomplished classical pianist so he brings a sort of "renaissance man" element to the team. The common thread is that all three men have a genuine interest in and curiosity about people. They love to ask questions and to get their clients talking about themselves.

The natural outcome of this attention to relationships is a feeling of mutual trust and, eventually, a business relationship that benefits both sides. They say their strategy is that it should not be an accident that someone gives them a referral.

Without question, the guys at 44 Financial see these relationships as friendships. They work hard to maintain these friendships, based on finding common ground around the most ordinary things — family, sports, card games, and having a lot of laughs. This is their version of developing Relational Capital. Remember Max said, "If you enjoy what you are doing, you'll never work a day in your life."

The laughing part may be one of the most important aspects of how they work. Bernie, Jeff, and Phil put a high value on balancing business with humor. Bernie says, "Making people laugh is important to us. People trust someone they can have a good laugh with. We fill our newsletter with humor and it all revolves around our clients. We get deals done and have fun in the process of doing it."

While developing relationships with the banks, attorneys and accountants is fundamental to the work of 44 Financial, the consequence of this is a second type of relationship: with the small business owner who gets referred to them. It's just as important that they succeed in this relationship so the transaction is completed smoothly and successfully and the referring parties are satisfied that the client has received good service.

In these relationships, Bernie, Jeff, and Phil become problem solvers. This is a very rewarding part of their work. Not only must they come up with viable options to provide financing under sometimes challenging circumstances, but they must be able to understand the people they are dealing with so well that they can guide them through tough decisions without offending them or causing them to lose face. These small business owners are mostly hard-working entrepreneurs — they typically have started their own businesses and feel they know their business and their situation better than anyone else. My friends know how to work sensitively with these business owners so that they feel their decision is truly his or her own, even when the options may be few.

The hardest part of this relationship is convincing the client that the higher interest rate they may have to pay is the best they can do in the situation and that the benefits of accepting this are far greater — as difficult as it may be — than the costs of NOT accepting it and not getting the financing they need. Jeff refers to himself in these relationships as the "Truth Doctor". He sees his job as telling the client the hard truth that has to be faced. He stresses that the terms are the fairest that can be achieved and that his firm earns no money until the deal actually closes. This helps relieve some of the stress, reduces the level of fear and helps build further trust. It's part of the art of helping the borrower arrive naturally at the conclusion that it's in his best interest to go ahead and do what the firm is proposing.

However, sometimes this relationship management has to be pretty direct. Bernie tells what he refers to as "the lawn chair story." One client they were working with was having a hard time accepting the idea he was going to have to go through with the deal they recommended. He was in denial and didn't want to go to closing. He said he would try to stay with his existing bank, even though this was the bank that had sent him to 44 Financial to solve his problem. Bernie reminded him they were the ones who were about to foreclose on his business. He said, "If you don't do something, they are going to have to put you out on the street!"

The customer still balked. The following is a great example of when you know that you have developed enough Relational Capital Gains to take a risk with a friend.

So in order to create a sense of reality for the customer, Bernie said, "Okay, here's what we'll do. Let's go down to Wal-Mart and buy a couple of lawn chairs and a cooler. We'll get a six-pack and we'll set up on the sidewalk outside your business tomorrow afternoon. Then, we'll be able to relax and kick back with a couple of beers while the sheriff sale starts and they dismantle your business, selling off the furniture, your computers and everything else. Unfortunately, you are out of options! There are no other steps to take."

The client, who knew Bernie for a long time, picked up the phone and called his bank to let them know he was going to close the deal with 44 Financial and basically save his business.

My friends also feel a real sense of responsibility and commitment in service to their clients. Jeff shared that there are times that their Relational Capital with the lender, the title companies, and sometimes even the IRS sometimes buys a "few extra days" to close a complicated loan before foreclosure or tax seizure.

As in the Bernie story above, Jeff emphasized that they have saved untold businesses and personal livelihoods from disaster by doing what has to be done, though some people they help have no real sense of how much the firm has saved them. He said, "It's like when a kid walks out on thin ice on a pond and you manage to pull him back before he falls through; they don't know the danger they were in and may or may not even thank you for it until sometime down the road."

One thing is certain, however. 44 Financial would never succeed — with the banks or with the small businesses that come to them for help — if they were not experts at developing their own brand of Relational Capital.

With the time, effort and sincerity they invest in these relationships, there are no individuals I have known in my entire career that have more positive Sound Bites in their customers' minds than these three guys. Their newsletter is filled with testimonials from their banking, legal and accounting friends as well as many of the small business owners who they have helped over the years. Mention their names to people you run into who know them and the first thing you notice is the smile that comes across their faces.

Every banker, lawyer, and accountant who continues to refer business, every friend who they keep in business, every laugh they have with a client over a game of golf or hand of pinochle, every phone call, personal note or holiday card, contributes to building the reserves of trust, goodwill and friendship that are the foundation of everything they have accomplished.

And they have accomplished a lot. They may not be ultra rich, but they are doing just fine, they are supporting their families, putting their kids through colleges, and most importantly, they are happy. They have created an attractive environment that draws friends into their world and ultimately produces business for the company. They have a great time every day running their business and people feel great about themselves when they are with these guys. They are ordinary people in an ordinary business, doing remarkable things for business owner friends in need of help, through understanding the value of relationships.

Chapter Summary

There are so many exciting ideas on building outstanding business relationships in this chapter that in order to summarize I would need to repeat much of the content. But, with that in mind, here's my attempt...

You know you've built solid Relational Capital when a banker is willing to send you on a 'blind date' with one of their customers.

CHAPTER TEN

Max's Legacy

Max passed away much too soon in our relationship and I suspect a lot of other people from all walks of life felt the same way. He had lived his life in service to his family and friends, and that is how he is remembered and appreciated. To me he was a special friend who took joy in making the ordinary unique. His life has continued to make my life a better one and will continue to do so for a long time to come.

One more short Max story

On one trip in early summer, Max's eyes were focused on the grassy strip down the middle of the highway.

"Aren't they remarkable?" he said.

By this point in our relationship, I knew to go with the flow when riding with Max.

"What's remarkable, Max, the flowers?"

Max rhapsodized for several minutes about the beauty of the wild-flowers that were sprouting in the median strip, as if Van Gogh himself had painted them. I, of course, had not even noticed them until he pointed them out. In those days, I was still pretty much squarely focused on the next deal, call, or contract.

"Yes Ed, and to think that the fact they're blooming there wasn't just an accident of nature; it was actually planned by our friends at the Highway Department!"

Of all my colleagues, acquaintances and, yes, friends, Max was the only one I knew who could or would go to such lengths to give credit to a group that was rarely appreciated for anything.

But this was how Max was: he always *appreciated the good in everything and everyone*. To him, expressing gratitude was much more than a matter of courtesy or manners; it was fundamental to his being. When he saw value in something, it was impossible for him not to express gratitude for it. And he truly valued his clients, their friendship and the business they gave him. On one side of his business card was his name and phone number, on the other side were simply the words, "Thank you."

Those who spent time with Max found that whatever they wanted to talk about, he would find it fresh and fascinating and would listen enthusiastically. Max never marginalized anyone. Their interests became his personal commitment. He was totally present, totally in the moment. He believed that so-called electronic conveniences serve primarily as distractions that keep people from being truly present with each other because they force you to be present with someone who isn't even there. While any other business person today might carry a cell phone, BlackBerry® or notebook computer, Max would still be carrying a small, spiral notebook.

Also, Max never patronized. You never had the feeling he was trying to get something. Rather, you had the feeling he *already had everything he wanted or needed* — the enjoyment he found in life and in each one of his friendships.

No wonder then that his business was so successful. Who wouldn't want to do business with someone so genuine, with such a strong sense of service to others?

Max's success, of course, didn't just happen by accident. It took a kind of crucible experience — his years in the Middle East during the hostage crisis — to force him to examine his priorities and redesign his life. I believe that he looked hard at what was truly important to him — his family, his friendships, his love of learning and his desire to serve others — and created a life that supported and nurtured these things and let him do it at his own pace and in his own style.

I'm embarrassed to admit this, but the full value of what I learned from Max didn't really sink in while he was still alive and I was spending time with him. Maybe I'm a bit of a slow study, but the fact is that during those years, I was so engrossed in my day-to-day work that I wasn't stepping back to see the big picture or notice the little extras, the subtleties of family life and business relationships, how important and connected they were. I was out of town at least half the time, away from my family, and always pushing for the next sale, the next new client, uh sorry, friend. When business is going well and things are basically calm on the home front, it's just too easy to be in denial about what you're missing or putting off.

All that changed for me one day when I got a phone call from Laurie.

She was not her usual self and I could sense something had happened. Our younger son Grant, who was 8 years old at the time, had fallen off a skateboard, hitting his head on the pavement, and the paramedics were on the way. She was directed to go to our local community college where the trauma helipad was located. The next ten minutes seemed like forever as I felt as though I had absolutely no control over what was occurring. I thought about what Grant must be going through with all of those strangers around him. Was he afraid? Was he even awake? Could he move his legs?

Ironically, my mind raced back to how peaceful I had felt in the hours after each of our children were born and I knew that everyone was okay. This moment was the complete opposite.

At the community college, I saw the helicopter and ambulance and all the surrounding commotion. I have to tell you, nothing could prepare me for something like this, no matter how many books I read on parenting, leadership or personal development. The next thing that I remember is Laurie looking down at me from the helicopter as she and Grant take off for the children's hospital.

When our older son Brett, now 15, and I arrived at the hospital, we found out that Grant had a severe concussion and some other complications that needed close monitoring. Six months later, Grant is still recovering, but indications are that he is just about out of the woods. Still, I just can't shake the memory of the whole scene. As I'm traveling on a flight one evening, I'm thinking about Max's journey from being an executive and surviving Middle East turmoil to making a new life driving a taxi and serving his friends.

I've started to reflect on my own sense of service and how I might find ways to contribute to helping my friends develop outstanding business relationships based on my experiences. I had long wanted to write a book on the importance of business relationships. But, it wasn't until my son lifted off that helipad that I developed more of a sense of urgency to "seize the day" as they say. As Grant was recuperating, I was suddenly compelled to share the experiences I'd had with Max and my re-appreciation of the essential qualities he championed. How these ideas applied universally to business and to life. With all my procrastinating, I guess you could say this book has been fifteen years in the making.

Now, neither Max nor I would suggest that you have to go through a crisis like we did to arrive at the conclusion that you need to consider putting the quality of your relationships and service to your friends ahead of a lot of other things. That's the way it happened for us, but another reason I wanted to write this book was to share that we can all think these issues through and get it right — *without all the drama.*

Max didn't go around telling people they should move away to learn a few life lessons. He simply wanted to share — in his unique, subtle, way — how he valued and appreciated the basic, good things in life, and his sense of how people should treat one another and conduct their business.

The journeys that I experienced with Max were deeply insightful:
Credibility — Mr. DeMarcantonio's Tomatoes and Dr. Fred;
Integrity — No Cutting in Line, and;
Authenticity — The Power of "I Don't Know."

Any one of these lessons would have been a substantial enough legacy for most people. The ideas are so simple, so basic — it's a wonder that I was unable to re-appreciate them more. Is it really so hard to "turn down" our electronic devices just as Max turned down the radio in the taxi, allow ourselves to listen to each other, find the common ground, to be honest and ethical, and to be genuinely ourselves, with no artifice? Max sure didn't think so.

Max called this phenomenon '*turning fares to friends.*' Fifteen years later, I call it '*developing Relational Capital.*' Either way, I believe that *How people know and regard you* is the most important element in any business relationship's path to success and to your own personal success. This element can be extremely abstract and rightfully experiential. So in keeping with that theme, here's a depiction of some phrases and ideas that I used throughout this book to help you re-appreciate the value of developing outstanding business relationships and ultimately create friendships in your business life.

...finding common ground

...friends in business   ...being yourself

...doing business on a handshake

...turning your "radio" down   ...earning trust

...enjoy what you're doing   ...asking for help

...how people know and regard you

...people enjoy having a good laugh

...reserving judgement   ...avoid marginalizing your friends

...integrity does not cut in line

...listening and remembering, saying "Thank You!"

...sleeping well at night   ...qualify for 'blind dates'

...creating a friendly business environment

...managing your time purposefully

...demonstrating sincere interest

...it's the little extras

Conclusion

There you have it, a great number of ways to develop Relational Capital that will amplify your personal net worth in life and business. Even better, building outstanding business relationships can begin **immediately** by using any one of these or by creating your own path. Consider your Sound Bites, seek common ground with someone, or reach out to that old friend who just fired you, because as Max might have put it —

"Whether at work or in your taxi — it's the little extras that friends do for each other that make all the difference."

Thanks very much for allowing me to share my experiences with you.

Your friend, Ed

Appendix A

My Greatest Hits from the Rock Stars of Leadership

Here's my short list of recommended additional reading from some really smart people. I hope that you can find time to enjoy at least a couple of these if you're looking for further, thoughtful analysis and truly creative thinking on subjects that complement what we've been discussing when turning 'fares to friends'.

6. *How to Win Friends and Influence People*, by Dale Carnegie – Pocket Books, a division of Simon Schuster, Inc.

   Written and published in 1936, the foundational principles in this work still apply today.

5. *Swim with the Sharks Without Being Eaten Alive*, by Harvey McKay – latest edition re-published by HarperBusiness Essentials, 2005.

   This is a great book written by a real business guy!

4. *Selling the Invisible*, by Harry Beckwith – Warner Books Inc, 1997.

   I included this book because while I read it looking for answers on marketing, I came away with much more. Beckwith shares a great deal about the importance of business relationships beyond any marketing work that I have found.

3.   *The Road Less Traveled*, by F. Scott Peck – A Touchstone Book, published by Simon and Schuster, 1978

This book was challenging for me to read due to the sheer depth of psychology and spirituality covered by Peck. But I found it incredibly powerful, rewarding, and well worth the effort.

2.   *The Seven Habits of Highly Effective People*, by Stephen R. Covey – A Fireside Book, published by Simon and Schuster

Written in 1989, this book is as powerful today as it was almost twenty years ago. An "evergreen" classic for all time.

AND the #1 book on my list of the Rock Stars of Leadership (drum roll please)…

1.   *Everything I Need to Know I Learned in Kindergarten*, by Robert Fulghum, published by Villard Books, a division of Random House, 1986

Max would certainly agree!

APPENDIX B

The "44" Profile

Try to find out as much about the customer and their product before you make the first call. Use resources like D&B, the Library, Suppliers the customer currently uses, and their Administrative Assistants.

Answer as many questions as possible the first time – then gradually fill in the rest.

Use the "44" for the customers you decide you want to do business with.

Review each profile monthly so you keep fresh the interests of your top customers and prospects.

Frequently send them info or whatever it takes to let them know you share in the same interests.

(continued on next page)

A. Customer

1. Name
   Nickname
   Title

2. Company name
   Address

3. Work phone
   Home phone

4. Birth date
   Birth place
   Hometown

5. Company owners
   Years in business

B. Education

6. College

7. Special degrees

8. High School

9. Extra curricular activities

10. Military service?   Y   N

C. Family

11. Marital status
    Spouse's name

12. Spouse's education

13. Spouse's interests

14. Children's names and ages

15. Children's schools

16. Children's interests

D. Business Background

17. Previous employment
    a. Company
        Location
        How long?
        Title
    b. Company
        Location
        How long?
        Title

18. Professional or Trade Association

19. What is the customer's attitude towards his company?

20. What is the customer's long-range business objectives?

E. Special Interests

21. Clubs

22. Politically active
    Party

23. Religion
    Active

F. Lifestyle

24. Does the customer drink alcohol?
    What does the customer drink?

25. Does the customer smoke cigars?

26. Favorite places to eat

27. Favorite menu

28. Hobbies and recreational interest

29. What does the customer like to read?

30. Sports interest

31. Vacation habits

32. Kind of car

G. The Customer and You

33. Does the customer feel any obligations to you, your company, or your competition?

    If so, what?

34. Are there any ethical considerations involved when you work with this customer?

35. What are the key problems as the customer sees them?

36. What are the priorities of management?

   Any conflicts?

H. The Product

37. What do they sell?

38. Biggest selling product

39. Average price
    range

40. Marketing territory

41. Their competition

42. Competitive advantage

43. Our competition

   What do they like?

   What do they dislike?

44. Additional notes

Roll the Credits

Chapter One

BlackBerry is a registered trademark of Research in Motion

Chapter Six

Microsoft is a registered trademark of Microsoft Corporation

Oracle is a registered trademark of Oracle Corporation

SAP is a registered trademark of SAP Corporation

Harvard Business Review "Wild West of Coaching", 2005

Chris Malone contributed to this chapter.

David Reibstein, PhD "Connecting Marketing Metrics to Financial Consequences", November 17, 2004

Chapter Eight

CEO Resources 2005 Survey

Chapter Nine

Based on interviews with the 44 Financial partners; Bernie McTamney, Jeff Sherry, and Phil Rapone

44 Financial is a trademark of 44 Financial/Pennant Mortgage; The "44" Profile is published with the permission of 44 Financial.